Xmas. 1995

To Dick & Lois,

In Remembrance of
your trip to Oz.

With love
Peter, Ann
& the kids,

BANJO PATERSON

In the Droving Days

Arthur Streeton, 1867–1943, Australia, *The purple noon's transparent might*, 1896, oil on canvas 121.8 x 122 cm. Purchased 1896. National Gallery of Victoria.

BANJO PATERSON

In the Droving Days

ILLUSTRATED WITH AUSTRALIAN LANDSCAPE PAINTINGS

Selected by Margaret Olds

NATIONAL
BOOK DISTRIBUTORS AND PUBLISHERS

Published by
National Book Distributors and Publishers
3/2 Aquatic Drive, Frenchs Forest, New South Wales, 2086, Australia

Devised and produced for the publishers by
Murray Child & Company Pty Ltd
64 Suffolk Avenue, Collaroy, New South Wales, 2097, Australia
Designed by Murray Child and Emma Seymour
This collection of poems and paintings
© Murray Child & Company Pty Ltd, 1994
© Design, Murray Child & Company Pty Ltd, 1994
Digital colour separation and film by Type Scan, Adelaide
Printed by Southbank Book, Melbourne

National Library of Australia Cataloguing-in-Publication Data

Paterson, A. B. (Andrew Barton), 1864–1941.
[Poems, Selections]. The Banjo Paterson collection.

ISBN 1 863436 023 2 (set).
ISBN 1 86436 030 5 (v.1).
ISBN 1 86436 031 3 (v.2).

1. Paterson, A. B. (Andrew Barton), 1864–1941. In the
droving days. II. Paterson, A. B. (Andrew Barton), 1864–
1941. Under sunny skies.
III. Olds, Margaret. IV. Title. V. Title: Under sunny skies.
VI. Title: In the droving days.

A821.2

Contents

Introduction

Andrew Barton Paterson ("the Banjo") is Australia's best known and best loved folk poet.

He was born at Narrambla, near Orange, in the heart of central New South Wales, on 17 February 1864. When he was aged seven, his family moved to Illalong, near Yass. He enjoyed a happy childhood in the bush, without experiencing the deprivation and hardship that Henry Lawson, the other great poet of the period, faced. Paterson's childhood was one of picnic races, polo club matches, horses and horsemanship, all fitted comfortably into a life on the land with its rhythms of the tasks of the seasons. He was surrounded by the characters of the times—bushmen, swagmen, horsemen, drovers and shearers. Bullock teams, gold escorts and bushrangers were part of everyday life. Today, the words themselves effortlessly evoke the spirit of an earlier time and a way of life, perhaps simpler than today's, that was crucial to the development of the Australian ethos.

In 1874 Paterson moved to Sydney to continue his education at Sydney Grammar School. He lived with his grandmother who actively fostered his developing love of verse. After leaving school he entered a legal office and in due course was admitted as a solicitor.

Paterson started to write verse while he was studying law. He took the pen-name "the Banjo" (after a racehorse owned by his family back in the bush), and submitted material to the *Bulletin*. This magazine was the vehicle for much of the best of verse, narrative prose, and journalism of the 1880s and 1890s, and it fostered the growing spirit of nationalism in this young country.

"The Man from Snowy River" was first published in the *Bulletin* in April 1890 to much acclaim. In the next few years a number of ballads for which Paterson is still famous, such as

"Clancy of the Overflow", "The Man from Ironbark" and "Saltbush Bill", appeared. The response was such that the publishers Angus & Robertson decided to publish a book of his verse and in 1895 *The Man from Snowy River and Other Verses* was released. Not only was the volume well received across the States of Australia, but it was also highly praised by critics in the United Kingdom. In Australia it was a runaway best-seller—the first edition sold out the week it was published. Indeed, today it is still Australia's best-selling verse collection.

Paterson's poems struck a chord in the hearts of Australians from all walks of life and they still draw that response today. His narrative verse with its galloping rhythms and rhymes has an innocent appeal and many of his poems overflow with humour and optimism. "Saltbush Bill", "The Man from Ironbark", Mulligan's Mare", and of course, "The Man from Snowy River" are typical of Paterson's best known work, while "Black Swans" and "Come-by-Chance" show his more introspective side.

MARGARET OLDS

Prelude

I have gathered these stories afar,
    In the wind and the rain,
In the land where the cattle camps are,
    On the edge of the plain.
On the overland routes of the west,
    When the watches were long,
I have fashioned in earnest and jest
    These fragments of song.

They are just the rude stories one hears
    In sadness and mirth,
The records of wandering years,
    And scant is their worth.
Though their merits indeed are but slight,
    I shall not repine,
If they give you one moment's delight,
    Old comrades of mine.

Duncan Cooper, 1813 or 14–1904, *Panorama of Challicum* No. VIII, watercolour 15.8 x 24 cm, *The Challicum Sketch Book*. National Library of Australia.

Come-by-Chance

As I pondered very weary o'er a volume long and dreary—
For the plot was void of interest—'twas that Postal Guide, in fact,
There I learnt the true location, distance, size, and population
Of each township, town, and village in the radius of the Act.

And I learnt that Puckawidgee stands beside the Murrumbidgee,
And that Booleroi and Bumble get their letters twice a year,
Also that the post inspector, when he visited Collector,
Closed the office up instanter, and re-opened Dungalear.

But my languid mood forsook me, when I found a name that
    took me,
Quite by chance I came across it—"Come-by-Chance" was what
    I read;
No location was assigned it, not a thing to help one find it,
Just an "N" which stood for northward, and the rest was all
    unsaid.

I shall leave my home, and forthward wander stoutly to the
    northward
Till I come by chance across it, and I'll straightway settle down,
For there can't be any hurry, nor the slightest cause for worry
Where the telegraph don't reach you nor the railways run to
    town.

And one's letters and exchanges come by chance across the
    ranges,
Where a wiry young Australian leads a pack horse once a
    week,

And the good news grows by keeping, and you're spared the
   pain of weeping
Over bad news when the mailman drops the letters in the
   creek.

But I fear, and more's the pity, that there's really no such city,
For there's not a man can find it of the shrewdest folk I know,
"Come-by-Chance", be sure it never means a land of fierce
   endeavour,
It is just the careless country where the dreamers only go.

Though we work and toil and hustle in our life of haste and
   bustle,
All that makes our life worth living comes unstriven for and
   free;
Man may weary and importune, but the fickle goddess
   Fortune
Deals him out his pain or pleasure careless what his worth may
   be.

All the happy times entrancing, days of sport and nights of
   dancing,
Moonlit rides and stolen kisses, pouting lips and loving glance:
When you think of these be certain you have looked behind
   the curtain,
You have had the luck to linger just a while in "Come-by-
   Chance".

Arthur Streeton, 1867–1943, Australia, *The purple noon's transparent might*, 1896, oil on canvas 121.8 x 122 cm. Purchased 1896. National Gallery of Victoria.

In the Droving Days

"Only a pound," said the auctioneer,
"Only a pound; and I'm standing here
Selling this animal, gain or loss.
Only a pound for the drover's horse;
One of the sort that was never afraid,
One of the boys of the Old Brigade;
Thoroughly honest and game, I'll swear,
Only a little the worst for wear;
Plenty as bad to be seen in town,
Give me a bid and I'll knock him down;
Sold as he stands, and without recourse,
Give me a bid for the drover's horse."

Loitering there in an aimless way
Somehow I noticed the poor old grey,
Weary and battered and screwed, of course,
Yet when I noticed the old grey horse,
The rough bush saddle, and single rein
Of the bridle laid on his tangled mane,
Straightway the crowd and the auctioneer
Seemed on a sudden to disappear,
Melted away in a kind of haze,
For my heart went back to the droving days.

Back to the road, and I crossed again
Over the miles of the saltbush plain—
The shining plain that is said to be
The dried-up bed of an inland sea,
Where the air so dry and so clear and bright
Refracts the sun with a wondrous light,

Edward Roper, *Yarding Stock for Branding; an old scrubber*, c.1855. This original oil is in the form of a Christmas card, inscribed: "A Merry Christmas", oil on academy board, 14.5 x 21.5 cm. National Library of Australia.

And out in the dim horizon makes
The deep blue gleam of the phantom lakes.
At dawn of day we would feel the breeze
That stirred the boughs of the sleeping trees,
And brought a breath of the fragrance rare
That comes and goes in that scented air;
For the trees and grass and the shrubs contain
A dry sweet scent on the saltbush plain.
For those that love it and understand,
The saltbush plain is a wonderland.
A wondrous country, where Nature's ways
Were revealed to me in the droving days.

We saw the fleet wild horses pass,
And the kangaroos through the Mitchell grass,
The emu ran with her frightened brood
All unmolested and unpursued.
But there rose a shout and a wild hubbub
When the dingo raced for his native scrub,
And he paid right dear for his stolen meals
With the drover's dogs at his wretched heels.
For we ran him down at a rattling pace,
While the packhorse joined in the stirring chase.
And a wild halloo at the kill we'd raise—
We were light of heart in the droving days.

'Twas a drover's horse, and my hand again
Made a move to close on a fancied rein.
For I felt the swing and the easy stride
Of the grand old horse that I used to ride
In drought or plenty, in good or ill,
That same old steed was my comrade still;
The old grey horse with his honest ways
Was a mate to me in the droving days.

A Singer of the Bush

There is waving of grass in the breeze
    And a song in the air,
And a murmur of myriad bees
    That toil everywhere.

There is scent in the blossom and bough,
　And the breath of the spring
Is as soft as a kiss on a brow—
　And springtime I sing.

There is drought on the land, and the stock
　Tumble down in their tracks
Or follow—a tottering flock—
　The scrub-cutter's axe.
While ever a creature survives
　The axes shall swing;
We are fighting with fate for their lives—
　And the combat I sing.

Tom Roberts, 1856–1931, Australia, *Evening, when the quiet east flushes faintly at the sun's last look*, 1887–88, oil on canvas 51 x 76.6 cm. W. H. Short Bequest 1944. National Gallery of Victoria.

Black Swans

As I lie at rest on a patch of clover
In the Western Park when the day is done,
I watch as the wild black swans fly over
With their phalanx turned to the sinking sun;
And I hear the clang of their leader crying
To a lagging mate in the rearward flying,
And they fade away in the darkness dying,
Where the stars are mustering one by one.

Oh! ye wild black swans, 'twere a world of wonder
For a while to join in your westward flight,
With the stars above and the dim earth under,
Through the cooling air of the glorious night.
As we swept along on our pinions winging,
We should catch the chime of a church-bell ringing,
Or the distant note of a torrent singing,
Or the far-off flash of a station light.

From the northern lakes with the reeds and rushes,
Where the hills are clothed with purple haze,
Where the bell-birds chime and the songs of thrushes
Make music sweet in the jungle maze,
They will hold their course to the westward ever,
Till they reach the banks of the old grey river,
Where the waters wash, and the reed-beds quiver
In the burning heat of the summer days.

Oh! ye strange wild birds, will ye bear a greeting
To the folk that live in that western land?
Then for every sweep of your pinions beating,
Ye shall bear a wish to the sunburnt band,

To the stalwart men who are stoutly fighting
With the heat and drought and the dust-storm smiting,
Yet whose life somehow has a strange inviting,
When once to the work they have put their hand.

Facing it yet! Oh, my friend stout-hearted,
What does it matter for rain or shine,
For the hopes deferred and the gain departed?
Nothing could conquer that heart of thine.
And thy health and strength are beyond confessing
As the only joys that are worth possessing.
May the days to come be as rich in blessing
As the days we spent in the auld lang syne.

I would fain go back to the old grey river,
To the old bush days when our hearts were light,
But, alas! those days they have fled for ever,
They are like the swans that have swept from sight.
And I know full well that the strangers' faces
Would meet us now in our dearest places;
For our day is dead and has left no traces
But the thoughts that live in my mind to-night.

There are folk long dead, and our hearts would sicken—
We would grieve for them with a bitter pain,
If the past could live and the dead could quicken,
We then might turn to that life again.
But on lonely nights we would hear them calling,
We should hear their steps on the pathways falling,
We should loathe the life with a hate appalling
In our lonely rides by the ridge and plain.

*　　　　*　　　　*

In the silent park is a scent of clover,
And the distant roar of the town is dead,
And I hear once more as the swans fly over
Their far-off clamour from overhead.
They are flying west, by their instinct guided,
And for man likewise is his fate decided,
And griefs apportioned and joys divided
By a mighty power with a purpose dread.

The Gundaroo Bullock

Oh, there's some that breeds the Devon that's
    as solid as a stone,
And there's some that breeds the brindle
    which they call the "Goulburn Roan";
But amongst the breeds of cattle there are
    very, very few
Like the hairy-whiskered bullock that they
    bred at Gundaroo.

Far away by Grabben Gullen, where the
    Murrumbidgee flows,
There's a block of broken countryside where
    no one ever goes;
For the banks have gripped the squatters, and
    the free selectors too,
And their stock are always stolen by the men
    of Gundaroo.

There came a low informer to the Grabben
    Gullen side,

Patrick William Maroney, *Police riding through gully*, ca 1894, oil on canvas 107 x 61cm.
National Library of Australia.

And he said to Smith the squatter, "You must saddle up and ride,
For your bullock's in the harness-cask of Morgan Donahoo—
He's the greatest cattle-stealer that abides in Gundaroo."

"Oh, ho!" said Smith, the owner of the Grabben Gullen run,
"I'll go and get the troopers by the sinking of the sun,
And down into his homestead tonight we'll take a ride,
With warrants to identify the carcase and the hide."

That night rode down the troopers, the squatter at their head,
They rode into the homestead, and pulled Morgan out of bed.
"Now, show to us the carcase of the bullock that you slew—
The great marsupial bullock that you killed in Gundaroo."

They peered into the harness-cask, and found it wasn't full,
But down among the brine they saw some flesh and bits of wool.
"What's this?" exclaimed the trooper—"an infant, I declare,"
Said Morgan, " 'Tis the carcase of an old man native bear.
I heard that ye were coming, so an old man bear I slew,
Just to give you kindly welcome to my home in Gundaroo.

"The times is something awful, as you can plainly see,
The banks have broke the squatters, and they've broke the likes
    of me;
We can't afford a bullock—such expense would never do—
So an old man bear for breakfast is a treat in Gundaroo."

And along by Grabben Gullen where the rushing river flows,
In the block of broken country where there's no one ever goes,
On the Upper Murrumbidgee they're a hospitable crew,
But you mustn't ask for "bullock" when you go to Gundaroo.

The Man from Ironbark

It was the man from Ironbark who struck the Sydney town,
He wandered over street and park, he wandered up and down.
He loitered here, he loitered there, till he was like to drop,
Until at last in sheer despair he sought a barber's shop.
" 'Ere! shave my beard and whiskers off, I'll be a man of mark,
I'll go and do the Sydney toff up home in Ironbark."

The barber man was small and flash, as barbers mostly are,
He wore a strike-your-fancy sash, he smoked a huge cigar:
He was a humorist of note and keen at repartee,
He laid the odds and kept a "tote", whatever that may be,
And when he saw our friend arrive, he whispered "Here's a lark!
Just watch me catch him all alive, this man from Ironbark."

There were some gilded youths that sat along the barber's wall.
Their eyes were dull, their heads were flat, they had no brains at
    all;
To them the barber passed the wink, his dexter eyelid shut,
"I'll make this bloomin' yokel think his bloomin' throat is cut."
And as he soaped and rubbed it in he made a rude remark:
"I s'pose the flats is pretty green up there in Ironbark."

A grunt was all reply he got; he shaved the bushman's chin,
Then made the water boiling hot and dipped the razor in.
He raised his hand, his brow grew black, he paused awhile to
    gloat,
Then slashed the red-hot razor-back across his victim's throat;
Upon the newly-shaven skin it made a livid mark—
No doubt it fairly took him in—the man from Ironbark.

He fetched a wild up-country yell might wake the dead to hear,
And though his throat, he knew full well, was cut from ear to
    ear,
He struggled gamely to his feet, and faced the murd'rous foe:
"You've done for me! you dog, I'm beat! one hit before I go!
I only wish I had a knife, you blessed murdering shark!
But you'll remember all your life, the man from Ironbark."

He lifted up his hairy paw, with one tremendous clout
He landed on the barber's jaw, and knocked the barber out.
He set to work with tooth and nail, he made the place a wreck;
He grabbed the nearest gilded youth, and tried to break his
    neck.
And all the while his throat he held to save his vital spark,
And "Murder! Bloody Murder!" yelled the man from Ironbark.

A peeler man who heard the din came in to see the show;
He tried to run the bushman in, but he refused to go.
And when at last the barber spoke, and said " 'Twas all in fun—
'Twas just a little harmless joke, a trifle overdone."
"A joke!" he cried, "By George, that's fine; a lively sort of lark;
I'd like to catch that murdering swine some night in Ironbark."

And now while round the shearing floor the list'ning shearers
    gape,
He tells the story o'er and o'er, and brags of his escape.
"Them barber chaps what keeps a tote, By George, I've had
    enough.
One tried to cut my bloomin' throat, but thank the Lord it's
    tough."
And whether he's believed or no, there's one thing to remark,
That flowing beards are all the go way up in Ironbark.

J. J. Hilder, Australia, 1881–1916, *The Crossroads*, 1910, watercolour on paper 73.5 x 53.7 cm.
Bequest of Dr George A. Brookes 1955. Art Gallery of New South Wales.

Mulligan's Mare

Oh, Mulligan's bar was the deuce of a place
To drink and to fight, and to gamble and race;
The height of choice spirits from near and from far
Were all concentrated on Mulligan's bar.

There was "Jerry the Swell", and the jockey boy Ned,
"Dog-bite-me"—so called from the shape of his head—
And a man whom the boys, in their musical slang,
Designed as the "Gaffer of Mulligan's Gang".

Now, Mulligan's Gang had a racer to show,
A bad 'un to look at, a good 'un to go;
Whenever they backed her you safely might swear
She'd walk in a winner, would Mulligan's mare.

But Mulligan, having some radical views,
Neglected his business and got "on the booze";
He took up with runners—a treacherous troop—
Who gave him away and he "fell in the soup".

And so it turned out on a fine summer day,
A bailiff turned up with a writ of *"fi fa"*;
He walked to the bar with a manner serene,
"I levy," said he, "in the name of the Queen."

Then Mulligan wanted, in spite of the law,
To pay out the bailiff with *"one* in the jaw",
He drew out to hit him, but, ere you could wink,
He changed his intentions and stood him a drink.

A great consulation there straightaway befell
'Twixt jockey boy Neddy and Jerry the Swell,
And the man with the head, who remarked, "Why, you bet!
Dog-bite-me!" said he, "but we'll diddle 'em yet.

George Rowe, *Victorian Race Meeting near Sunbury*, 1858, watercolour 67.9 x 167.6 cm.
Dixson Galleries, Mitchell Library, Sydney.

"We'll slip out the mare from her stall in a crack,
And put in her place the old broken-down hack;
The hack is so like her, I'm ready to swear
The bailiff will think he has Mulligan's mare.

"So out with the racer and in with the screw,
We'll show him what Mulligan's talent can do;
And if he gets nasty and dares to say much
I'll knock him as stiff as my grandmother's crutch."

Then off to the town went the mare and the lad;
The bailiff came out, never dream't he was "had";
But marched to the stall with a confident air—
"I levy," said he, "upon Mulligan's mare."

He never would let her go out of his sight,
He watched her by day and he watched her by night,
For races were coming away in the west
And Mulligan's mare had a chance with the best.

And, thinking to quietly serve his own ends,
He sent off a wire to some bookmaking friends:
"Get all you can borrow, beg, snavel, or snare
And lay the whole lot against Mulligan's mare."

The races came round, and a crowd on the course
Were laying the mare till they made themselves hoarse,
And Mulligan's party, with ardour intense,
They backed her for pounds and for shillings and pence.

And think of the grief of the bookmaking host
At sound of the summons to go to the post—
For down to the start with her thoroughbred air
As fit as a fiddle pranced Mulligan's mare!

They started, and off went the boy to the front,
He cleared out at once, and he made it a hunt;
He steadied as rounding the corner they wheeled,
Then gave her her head and she smothered the field.

The race put her owner right clear of his debts,
He landed a fortune in stakes and in bets,
He paid the old bailiff the whole of his pelf,
And gave him a hiding to keep for himself.

So all you bold sportsmen take warning, I pray,
Keep clear of the running, you'll find it don't pay;
For the very best rule that you'll hear in a week—
Is never to bet on a thing that can speak.

And whether you're lucky or whether you lose,
Keep clear of the cards and keep clear of the booze,
And fortune in season will answer your prayer,
And send you a flyer like Mulligan's mare.

The Man from Snowy River

There was movement at the station, for the word had passed around
That the colt from old Regret had got away,
And had joined the wild bush horses—he was worth a thousand
    pound,
So all the cracks had gathered to the fray.
All the tried and noted riders from the stations near and far
Had mustered at the homestead overnight,
For the bushmen love hard riding where the wild bush horses are,
And the stock-horse snuffs the battle with delight.

There was Harrison, who made his pile when Pardon won the cup,
The old man with his hair as white as snow;
But few could ride beside him when his blood was fairly up—
He would go wherever horse and man could go.
And Clancy of the Overflow came down to lend a hand,
No better horseman ever held the reins;
For never horse could throw him while the saddle girths would
    stand,
He learnt to ride while droving on the plains.

And one was there, a stripling on a small and weedy beast,
He was something like a racehorse undersized,
With a touch of Timor pony—three parts thoroughbred at least—
And such as are by mountain horsemen prized.
He was hard and tough and wiry—just the sort that won't say die—
There was courage in his quick impatient tread;
And he bore the badge of gameness in his bright and fiery eye,
And the proud and lofty carriage of his head.

But so slight and weedy, one would doubt his power to stay,
And the old man said, "That horse will never do

For a long and tiring gallop—lad, you'd better stop away,
Those hills are far too rough for such as you."
So he waited sad and wistful—only Clancy stood his friend—
"I think we ought to let him come," he said;
"I warrant he'll be with us when he's wanted at the end,
For both his horse and he are mountain bred.

"He hails from Snowy River, up by Kosciusko's side,
Where the hills are twice as steep and twice as rough,
Where a horse's hoofs strike firelight from the flint stones every
    stride,
The man that holds his own is good enough.
And the Snowy River riders on the mountains make their home,
Where the river runs those giant hills between;
I have seen full many horsemen since I first commenced to roam,
But nowhere yet such horsemen have I seen."

So he went—they found the horses by the big mimosa clump—
They raced away towards the mountain's brow,
And the old man gave his orders, "Boys, go at them from the jump,
No use to try for fancy riding now.
And, Clancy, you must wheel them, try and wheel them to the right.
Ride boldly, lad, and never fear the spills,
For never yet was rider that could keep the mob in sight,
If once they gain the shelter of those hills."

So Clancy rode to wheel them—he was racing on the wing
Where the best and boldest riders take their place,
And he raced his stockhorse past them, and he made the ranges
    ring
With stockwhip, as he met them face to face.
Then they halted for a moment, while he swung the dreaded lash,
But they saw their well-loved mountain full in view,

C. Martens (signed, lower right), *View from the Main Dividing Range*, watercolour 19.7 x 29.5 cm. Mitchell Library, Sydney.

And they charged beneath the stockwhip with a sharp and sudden
  dash,
And off into the mountain scrub they flew.

Then fast the horsemen followed, where the gorges deep and black
Resounded to the thunder of their tread,
And the stockwhips woke the echoes, and they fiercely answered
  back
From cliffs and crags that beetled overhead.
An upward, ever upward, the wild horses held their sway,
Where mountain ash and kurrajong grew wide;
And the old man muttered fiercely, "We may bid the mob good day,
No man can hold them down the other side."

When they reached the mountain's summit, even Clancy took a
     pull,
It well might make the boldest hold their breath,
The wild hop scrub grew thickly, and the hidden ground was full
Of wombat holes, and any slip was death.
But the man from Snowy River let the pony have his head,
And he swung his stockwhip round and gave a cheer,
And he raced him down the mountain like a torrent down its bed,
While the others stood and watched in very fear.

He sent the flint stones flying, but the pony kept his feet,
He cleared the fallen timbers in his stride,
And the man from Snowy River never shifted in his seat—
It was grand to see that mountain horseman ride.
Through the stringybarks and saplings, on the rough and broken
     ground,
Down the hillside at a racing pace he went;
And he never drew the bridle till he landed safe and sound,
At the bottom of that terrible descent.

He was right among the horses as they climbed the further hill
And the watchers on the mountain standing mute,
Saw him ply the stockwhip fiercely, he was right among them still,
As he raced across the clearing in pursuit.
Then they lost him for a moment, where two mountain gullies met
In the ranges, but a final glimpse reveals
On a dim and distant hillside the wild horses racing yet,
With the man from Snowy River at their heels.

And he ran them single-handed till their sides were white with foam.
He followed like a bloodhound in their track,
Till they halted cowed and beaten, then he turned their heads for
     home,

And alone and unassisted brought them back.
But his hardy mountain pony he could scarcely raise a trot,
He was blood from hip to shoulder from the spur;
But his pluck was still undaunted, and his courage fiery hot,
For never yet was mountain horse a cur.

And down by Kosciusko, where the pine clad ridges raise
Their torn and rugged battlements on high,
Where the air is clear as crystal, and the white stars fairly blaze
At midnight in the cold and frosty sky,
And where around The Overflow the reed beds sweep and sway
To the breezes, and the rolling plains are wide,
The man from Snowy River is a household word today,
And the stockmen tell the story of his ride.

The Uplift

When the drays are bogged and sinking, then it's no use
    sitting thinking,
  You must put the teams together and must double-bank the pull.
When the crop is light and weedy, or the fleece is burred and seedy,
  Then the next year's crop and fleeces may repay you to the full.

  So it's lift her, Johnny, lift her,
  Put your back in it and shift her,
While the jabber, jabber, jabber of the politicians flows.
  If your nag's too poor to travel
  Then get down and scratch the gravel
For you'll get there if you walk it—if you don't, you'll feed the
    crows.

Shall we waste our time debating with a grand young country
        waiting
    For the plough and for the harrow and the lucerne and the
        maize?
For it's work alone will save us in the land that fortune gave us
    There's no crop but what we'll grow it; there's no stock but
        what we'll raise.

    When the team is bogged and sinking
    Then it's no use sitting thinking.
There's a roadway up the mountain that the old black leader
        knows:
    So it's lift her, Johnny, lift her,
    Put your back in it and shift her,
Take a lesson from the bullock—he goes slowly, but he goes!

Nicholas Chevalier, 1828–1902, Australia, *The Buffalo Ranges*,1864, oil on canvas 129.5 x 180.3 cm. Purchased with the assistance of a Government Grant 1864. National Gallery of Victoria.

Saltbush Bill's Second Fight

The news came down on the Castlereagh, and went to the
    world at large,
That twenty thousand travelling sheep, with Saltbush Bill in
    charge,
Were drifting down from a dried-out run to ravage the
    Castlereagh;
And the squatters swore when they heard the news, and
    wished they were well away:
For the name and the fame of Saltbush Bill were over the
    country side
For the wonderful way that he fed his sheep, and the dodges
    and tricks he tried.
He would lose his way on a Main Stock Route, and stray to the
    squatters' grass;
He would come to the run with the boss away, and swear he
    had leave to pass;
And back of all and behind it all, as well the squatters knew,
If he had to fight, he would fight all day, so long as his sheep
    got through:
But this is the story of Stingy Smith, the owner of Hard Times Hill,
And the way that he chanced on a fighting man to reckon with
    Saltbush Bill.

              *   *   *

'Twas Stingy Smith on his stockyard sat, and prayed for an
    early Spring,
When he stared at sight of a clean-shaved tramp, who walked
    with a jaunty swing;
For a clean-shaved tramp with a jaunty walk a-swinging along
    the track

Is as rare a thing as a feathered frog on the desolate roads out
    back.
So the tramp he made for the travellers' hut, and asked could
    he camp the night;
But Stingy Smith had a bright idea, and he said to him, "Can
    you fight?"
"Why, what's the game?" said the clean-shaved tramp, as he
    looked at him up and down—
"If you want a battle, get off that fence, and I'll kill you for
    half-a-crown!
But, Boss, you'd better not fight with me, it wouldn't be fair
    nor right;
I'm Stiffener Joe, from the Rocks Brigade, and I killed a man
    in a fight:
I served two years for it, fair and square, and now I'm a
    trampin' back,
To look for a peaceful quiet life away on the outside track—"
"Oh, it's not myself, but a drover chap," said Stingy Smith with
    glee;
"A bullying fellow, called Saltbush Bill—and you are the man
    for me.
He's on the road with his hungry sheep, and he's certain to
    raise a row,
For he's bullied the whole of the Castlereagh till he's got them
    under cow—
Just pick a quarrel and raise a fight, and leather him good and
    hard,
And I'll take good care that his wretched sheep don't wander
    half a yard.
It's a five-pound job if you belt him well—do anything short of
    kill,
For there isn't a beak on the Castlereagh will fine you for
    Saltbush Bill."

Arthur Streeton, 1867–1943, Australia, *The land of the golden fleece*, 1926, oil on canvas 49.9 x 76.5 cm. Bequeathed by W. C. C. Cain 1950. National Gallery of Victoria.

"I'll take the job," said the fighting man; "and hot as this cove
   appears,
He'll stand no chance with a bloke like me, what's lived on the
   game for years;
For he's maybe learnt in a boxing school, and sparred for a
   round or so,
But I've fought all hands in a ten-foot ring each night in a travelling show;
They earned a pound if they stayed three rounds, and they
   tried for it every night—
In a ten-foot ring! Oh, that's the game that teaches a bloke to
   fight,
For they'd rush and clinch, it was Dublin Rules, and we drew
   no colour line;

And they all tried hard for to earn the pound, but they got no
    pound of mine:
If I saw no chance in the opening round I'd slog at their wind,
    and wait
Till an opening came—and it *always* came—and I settled 'em,
    sure as fate;
Left on the ribs and right on the jaw—and, when the chance
    comes, *make sure!*
And it's there a professional bloke like me gets home on an
    amateur:
For it's my experience every day, and I make no doubt it's
    yours,
That a third-class pro is an over-match for the best of the
    amateurs—"
"Oh, take your swag to the travellers' hut," said Smith, "for you
    waste your breath;
You've a first-class chance, if you lose the fight, of talking your
    man to death.
I'll tell the cook you're to have your grub, and see that you eat
    your fill,
And come to the scratch all fit and well to leather this Saltbush Bill."

               *   *   *

'Twas Saltbush Bill, and his travelling sheep were wending
    their weary way
On the Main Stock Route, through the Hard Times Run, on
    their six-mile stage a day;
And he strayed a mile from the Main Stock Route, and started
    to feed along,
And, when Stingy Smith came up, Bill said that the Route was
    surveyed wrong;
And he tried to prove that the sheep had rushed and strayed
    from their camp at night,

But the fighting man he kicked Bill's dog, and of course that
meant a fight:
So they sparred and fought, and they shifted ground, and
never a sound was heard
But the thudding fists on their brawny ribs, and the seconds'
muttered word,
Till the fighting man shot home his left on the ribs with a
mighty clout,
And his right flashed up with a half-arm blow—and Saltbush
Bill "went out".
He fell face down, and towards the blow; and their hearts with
fear were filled,
For he lay as still as a fallen tree, and they thought that he
must be killed.

So Stingy Smith and the fighting man, they lifted him from
the ground,
And sent to home for a brandy flask, and they slowly fetched
him round;
But his head was bad, and his jaw was hurt—in fact, he could
scarcely speak—
So they let him spell till he got his wits, and he camped on the
run for a week,
While the travelling sheep went here and there, wherever they
liked to stray,
Till Saltbush Bill was fit once more for the track to the
Castlereagh.

Then Stingy Smith he wrote a note, and gave to the fighting
man:
'Twas writ to the boss of the neighbouring run, and thus the
missive ran:

"The man with this is a fighting man, one Stiffener Joe by name;
He came near murdering Saltbush Bill, and I found it a costly
   game:
But it's worth your while to employ the chap, for there isn't
   the slightest doubt
You'll have no trouble from Saltbush Bill while this man hangs
   about—"
But an answer came by the next week's mail, with news that
   might well appal:
"The man you sent with a note is not a fighting man at all!
He has shaved his beard, and has cut his hair, but I spotted
   him at a look;
He is Tom Devine, who has worked for years for Saltbush Bill
   as cook.
Bill coached him up in the fighting yarn, and taught him the
   tale by rote,
And they shammed to fight, and they got your grass and divided your five-pound note.
'Twas a clean take-in, and you'll find it wise—'twill save you a
   lot of pelf—
When next you're hiring a fighting man, just fight him a
   round yourself."

And the teamsters out on the Castlereagh, when they meet
   with a week of rain,
And the waggon sinks to its axle-tree, deep down in the black
   soil plain,
When the bullocks wade in a sea of mud, and strain at the
   load of wool,
And the cattle dogs at the bullocks' heels are biting to make
   them pull,
When the offside driver flays the team, and curses them while
   he flogs,

And the air is thick with the language used, and the clamour
   of men and dogs—
The teamsters say, as they pause to rest and moisten each hairy
   throat,
They wish they could swear like Stingy Smith when he read
   that neighbour's note.

The Old Australian Ways

The London lights are far abeam
   Behind a bank of cloud,
Along the shore the gas lights gleam,
   The gale is piping loud;
And down the Channel, groping blind,
   We drive her through the haze
Towards the land we left behind—
The good old land of "never mind",
   And old Australian ways.

The narrow ways of English folk
   Are not for such as we;
They bear the long-accustomed yoke
   Of staid conservancy:
But all our roads are new and strange
   And through our blood there runs
The vagabonding love of change
That drove us westward of the range
   And westward of the suns.

The city folk go to and fro
   Behind a prison's bars,

They never feel the breezes blow
    And never see the stars;
They never hear in blossomed trees
    The music low and sweet
Of wild birds making melodies,
Nor catch the little laughing breeze
    That whispers in the wheat.

Our fathers came of roving stock
    That could not fixed abide:
And we have followed field and flock
    Since e'er we learnt to ride;
By miner's camp and shearing shed,
    In land of heat and drought,
We followed where our fortunes led,
With fortune always on ahead
    And always further out.

The wind is in the barley grass,
    The wattles are in bloom;
The breezes greet us as they pass
    With honey-sweet perfume;
The parakeets go screaming by
    With flash of golden wing,
And from the swamp the wild ducks cry
Their long-drawn note of revelry,
    Rejoicing at the spring.

So throw the weary pen aside
    And let the papers rest,
For we must saddle up and ride
    Towards the blue hill's breast;
And we must travel far and fast

Across their rugged maze,
To find the Spring of Youth at last,
And call back from the buried past
    The old Australian ways.

When Clancy took the drover's track
    In years of long ago,
He drifted to the outer back
    Beyond the Overflow;
By rolling plain and rocky shelf,
    With stockwhip in his hand,
He reached at last, oh lucky elf,
The Town of Come-and-Help-Yourself
    In Rough-and-Ready Land.

Unknown artist, *Lake Borambeet—'The Stockman'*. National Library of Australia.

41

And if it be that you would know
    The tracks he used to ride,
Then you must saddle up and go
    Beyond the Queensland side—
Beyond the reach of rule or law,
    To ride the long day through,
In Nature's homestead—filled with awe:
You then might see what Clancy saw
    And know what Clancy knew.

The Silent Shearer

Weary and listless, sad and slow,
    Without any conversation,
Was a man that worked on The Overflow,
    The butt of the shed and station.

The shearers christened him Noisy Ned,
    With an alias "Silent Waters",
But never a needless word he said
    In the hut, or the shearers' quarters.

Which caused annoyance to Big Barcoo,
    The shed's unquestioned ringer,
Whose name was famous Australia through
    As a dancer, fighter and singer.

He was fit for the ring, if he'd had his rights
    As an agent of devastation;
And the number of men he had killed in fights
    Was his principal conversation.

John Mather, Australia, 1848–1916, *A Woolshed, Victoria* 1889, oil on canvas 49.7 x 89.7 cm. Purchased 1971. Art Gallery of New South Wales.

"I have known blokes go to their doom," said he,
    "Through actin' with haste and rashness:
But the style that this Noisy Ned assumes,
    It's nothing but silent flashness.

"We may just be dirt, from his point of view,
    Unworthy a word in season;
But I'll make him talk like a cockatoo
    Or I'll get him to show the reason."

Was it chance or fate, that King Condamine,
    A king who had turned black tracker,
Had captured a baby porcupine,
    Which he swapped for a "fig tobacker"?

With the porcupine in the Silent's bed
    The shearers were quite elated,
And the things to be done, and the words to be said,
    Were anxiously awaited.

With a screech and a howl and an eldritch cry
    That nearly deafened his hearers
He sprang from his bunk, and his fishy eye
    Looked over the laughing shearers.

He looked them over and he looked them through
    As a cook might look through a larder;
"Now, Big Barcoo, I must pick on you,
    You're big, but you'll fall the harder."

Now, the silent man was but slight and thin
    And of middleweight conformation,
But he hung one punch on the Barcoo's chin
    And it ended the altercation.

"You've heard of the One-round Kid," said he,
    "That hunted 'em all to shelter?
The One-round Finisher—that was me,
    When I fought as the Champion Welter.

"And this Barcoo bloke on his back reclines
    For being a bit too clever,
For snakes and wombats and porcupines
    Are nothing to me whatever.

"But the golden rule that I've had to learn
    In the ring, and for years I've tried it,
Is only to talk when it comes your turn,
    And never to talk outside it."

Old Schooldays

Awake, of Muse, the echoes of a day
Long past, the ghosts of mem'ries manifold—
Youth's memories that once were green and gold
But now, alas, are grim and ashen grey.

The drowsy schoolboy wakened up from sleep,
First stays his system with substantial food,
Then off for school with tasks half understood,
Alas, alas, that cribs should be so cheap!

The journey down to town—'twere long to tell
The storm and riot of the rabble rout;

L. Stalker, *Early settler's home, Victoria*, 1908. National Library of Australia.

The wild Walpurgis revel in and out
That made the ferry boat a floating hell.

What time the captive locusts fairly roared:
And bulldog ants, made stingless with a knife,
Climbed up the seats and scared the very life
From timid folk, who near jumped overboard.

The hours of lessons—hours with feet of clay
Each hour a day, each day more like a week:
While hapless urchins heard with blanched cheek
The words of doom "Come in on Saturday".

The master gowned and spectacled, precise,
Trying to rule by methods firm and kind
But always just a little bit behind
The latest villainy, the last device,

Born of some smoothfaced urchin's fertile brain
To irritate the hapless pedagogue,
And first involve him in a mental fog
Then "have" him with the same old tale again.

The "bogus" fight that brought the sergeant down
To that dark corner by the old brick wall,
Where mimic combat and theatric brawl
Made noise enough to terrify the town.

But on wet days the fray was genuine,
When small boys pushed each other in the mud
And fought in silence till thin streams of blood
Their dirty faces would incarnadine.

The football match or practice in the park
With rampant hoodlums joining in the game
Till on one famous holiday there came
A gang that seized the football for a lark.

Then raged the combat without rest or pause,
Till one, a hero, Hawkins unafraid
Regained the ball, and later on displayed
His nose knocked sideways in his country's cause.

Before the mind quaint visions rise and fall,
Old jokes, old sports, old students dead and gone:
And some that lead us still, while some toil on
As rank and file, but "Grammar" children all.

And he, the pilot, who has laid the course
For all to steer by, honest, unafraid—
Truth is his beacon light, so he has made
The name of the old School a living force.